I0098045

DEAR BLACK MEN:

I Love You

KIMBERLY HUMPHREY

Palmetto Publishing Group, LLC
Charleston, SC

ISBN-13: 978-1-944313-06-7
ISBN-10: 1-944313-06-0

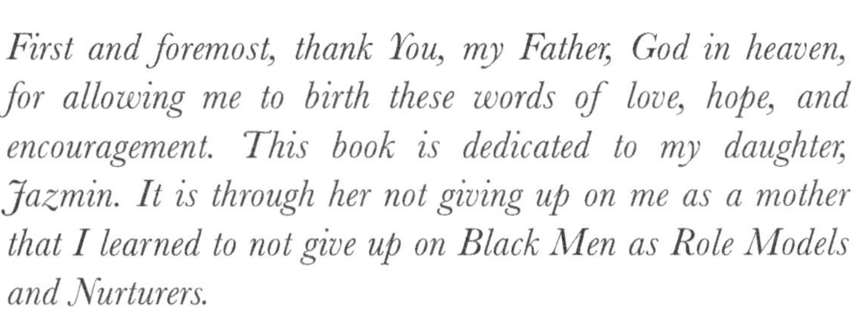

First and foremost, thank You, my Father, God in heaven, for allowing me to birth these words of love, hope, and encouragement. This book is dedicated to my daughter, Jazmin. It is through her not giving up on me as a mother that I learned to not give up on Black Men as Role Models and Nurturers.

For Jazmin

They told me you were dead.
They said you had no life.
But I would give everything
to make you turn out right.
When you came, there was no cry.
When you came, there was no light.
But I would give everything
just to hear you sigh.
He cut you out of me.
He took you still in new birth.
But I would give everything
to see your eyes, to be the first.
Four and a half hours later,
four and a half hours of not knowing.
But I would give everything
to feel your breath flowing.
Finally, you opened your eyes,
finally, you live!
But I would still give everything,
everything I would give.

Table of Contents

Preface

Prayer for My Unknown Future Husband

In the name of Jesus, Lord, I seek You to help me to be the help-meet that he will need. I pray that where he lacks, I fill. And where I lack, he fills. Lord please let finances more than cover our finances and let us live a comfortable life. I do not know what he is going through right now, but God, I ask that You cover him and put a hedge of protection around him. Safeguard him from the enemy who only seeks to kill, steal, and destroy. Lord, I ask if his body is not healthy, You will come in and touch his affliction to make him heal. You said, by Your stripes, we are healed, God. I trust You to heal him. The heavy burden he feels all around him, Lord, remind him You are to carry our burdens. Help him to be the joyous man of God he is destined to be. God, I ask all of this in Jesus name, Amen.

PART 1:

Black Man

Black Man

His strength is undeniable.
His passion is unquenchable
except by the woman destined to be his mate.
His thoughts are fluid
and process calculating.
When his voice speaks, I listen.
When his eyes speak, I obey.
There is only One placed above him
and he also bows to the One's feet.
I treasure the time alone
and brag about every good time with him.
I long for the moment he says my name
because he knows every nuance of me.
I appreciate his candor
and I am devoted to his needs.
His emotions run very deep,
his love is unbreakable.
He is a Black Man.
The black man will always be my King. He will also go in front of me, he is my rock, he protects me, and he calms my fears and caresses my inner beauty. I owe black men; I am in love with them. The way their skin looks next to mine, and the way they look at me, just that look, mmmm. Black men can get it, ALL of it!

I Like That

I like that.
I like what I see.
From the swaying to the beat,
to the rhythmic feet.
I like that.
I like what I see.
From the way glances are thrown at me
To the way that I throw them back.
I like that.
I like what I see.
Sitting here in this reggae infused atmosphere, listening to the sounds of jumping beats and bumpin' lyrics, I look across the room and I am pleasantly surprised. Have I ever seen someone so pleasing to my eyes? The Brotha has it. He. Has. The. IT! The IT that has me and it is not so easy to get me.
I enjoy the sight that my eyes behold.
Standing, laughing, talking to his boys…boy, does he have me. When drinks are passed around, he takes a pass, and pulls out his own bottle, light…sparkling… water. NOW, I am in deeper.
I want, no, I NEED to see more of the surprises that are in store for me.
He knows I am glancing.
He knows I am watching to see what comes next. Next

to come, it seems, is me.
Ooohhhh they just switched the music to neo-soul.
I stand with my girls, laughing, talking and enjoying the smooth sounds of the melodic beats because they seem to move…my…feet. Oh, wait, is that my jam???
I glance in his direction but he has disappeared. But wait… I whisper softly 'oohhh whee who is that behind me'? I hear softly spoken words in my ear, 'dance with me…please'. No need to turn around because he…and I…already know the answer.
'Next Lifetime' by Erykah Badu is right on time in this life-time. Right now this lifetime belongs to the dance floor and us. It seems as if we are gliding, swaying… shhh, no talking…just feeling. Feeling this music and the hypnotic notes slide around, up and down, pushing us closer. We still have not looked into each other's eyes.
Next song by Bilal 'Soul Sista" and yes, I am but I want to know how deep am I into your soul?
We look into each other eyes and I cannot deny that this-brotha-makes-me-want-to-flyyyy!
Did my heart just stop?
Did I just stumble?
Was that my breath? Caught in my throat?
Did that just happen to me???
Did he just happen to me?
Ohhhh his breath smells like apples, so fresh, no taint, nothing unclean. My body spray smells of peaches.

Hmph, what a combo! Nothing wrong with a healthy cock…tail for us.
I am taken aback, blown away.
Blown away because this brotha is diggin' me, the way I …am…him…

Standing Tall

Watching you up there
standing proud,
standing fine,
makes me so much more proud
to say you are mine.
Your gestures,
the way you speak,
captivates an audience,
makes all the ladies weak.
You are like a subtle fine wine,
only better with time.
Your presence is so strong
and your back is so firm.
The way the words fly from your lips
puts a tingle in my hips.
Come be with me
until the end and forever.
You are my black man
and I… am your heaven.

Fruit Salad

Strawberries and cherries, that's what I have for you. My golden box is ripe and juicy, take a sniff, and take a taste, right there, below my waist. Let me rub this strawberry nub across your lips. Reach for this juicy peach that has juices so sweet. Bust my cherry; you know it's your favorite berry.

Fajita

Ohhh Papi, you make me feel like a sexy Mami! I am hot, on fire, I sizzle when I taste your drizzle. Papi, come let Mami feed you. Open your mouth, open wide, let me slide my hot juices inside.

Fudge

Fudge?
Is lickable from the left to the right nipple.
Is suckable from the tip of the shaft
to the bottom of the ball sac.
There is nothing sexier than seeing thick brown fudge
spread on a thick brown man.

French Toast

Open your mouth, let me feed you. I want to dangle this in front of your face. A golden, toasty brown, sweet clit for you to lick, for you to eat, take a bite…

Glaze

That chocolate glaze of smooth skin.
The sweet drip-drops of nectar from his….
Chin.
His flavor is perfection to me.
I'm addicted, I can't breathe.
I want to taste him in every way.
Every hour of my day.

S.A.L.T. – Sex At Lunch Time

Her

Thanks for picking me up for lunch today. I really enjoy your company. Put the windows down, let my hair blow free. Where are we going? What are we eating? Salt? Salt?? Okay, surprise me!

Him

S – Scoot down, let me see the pearl, it's hidden in the box of gold
A - Allow me to feast, let me munch on that edible flower, you better take hold
L – Licking up, licking down, I'm licking round and round
T – Tell me, talk to me, I need to hear the moans, I get lost in the sound

Her

Thank you for lunch today; I had a really good time. On the next lunch date, keep the same menu, but add a sprinkle of lime.

Clues and Tips

Part. 1

Do Men Pay Attention to...A KISS???

Kisses, when they are soulful and deep, can make your soul cry and shed tears of joy. A kiss can touch you in such a profound, spiritual way, as if a secret place long hidden is now opened for the first time. Life, as you know it, will never be the same again. A kiss can put you in touch with the essence of your being. The warmth of passion exchanged when tongues touch to express the fervor of desire, exploring the soft flesh that will soon trigger the sounds of sighs and moans, followed by murmurs of short… shallow…breaths. It feels like your skin is alive! Almost as if your entire body is on fire! Kissing is an art form few have mastered. It requires patience, a certain rhythm, an unselfish desire to find out what will give your lover pleasure while inhaling the intoxicating aroma of their sensuality. You are learning what they need to feed their spirit. You can make love to a woman when you are kissing her soul, wetting her appetite for all the kisses to come. All you have to do is pay special attention. A kiss will tell you what a woman wants. A kiss has a beautiful sensual language all its own. Telling you exactly where you need to touch your woman, turning her on long after the kiss is over…

Part. 2

Can Men Touch Without having a Motive?

Can you simply touch your woman with no hidden intention, with nothing sexual as the motive? Can you walk up behind your woman and gently massage her shoulders and place a soft kiss upon her cheek right before you whisper "Good morning"? That itself will cause your woman to want, need, and desire you in a way only "sexual" touching cannot. Men have to learn how to hold, caress, and comfort their women with the strength of their arms and warmth of their masculinity. Your woman should be able to simply lie with and/or under you without being mauled five minutes later. Emotional touch yields far better results than sexual touch alone.

Attention without Obligation…

Attention without obligation is a simple habit to form. It means to be attentive to your woman without feeling that you have to be. Men tend to show affection and/or some form of attention after a heated discussion has taken place about why he doesn't already. This will last until the effects of the discussion wear off, then he's back to his normal way of response. It is in a man's nature to show real attention to things most important to him. They pay attention to their favorite sports teams, though they have no obligation to the team; yet, they can't pay that same degree of attention to their women.

Part. 3

18 Simple Reminders:
1. Kiss her
2. Hold her
3. Compliment her
4. Caress her
5. Listen to her
6. Laugh with her
7. Understand her
8. Make her smile
9. Make her scream your name
10. Appreciate her
11. Surprise her
12. Arouse her
13. Educate her
14. Acknowledge her
15. Accept her
16. Believe in her
17. Want her
18. Above all others…love her.

Part. 4

What a Good Relationship Should be

1. Laughing together
2. Take showers with her…wash his shoulders
3. Read to her when she's sick
3. Deep wet kisses every chance you get
4. Sleep eye-to-eye
5. Rub her feet...girls rub his too!
5. Cook food together
6. Sing to her in the car
7. Kiss him in the rain
8. Stare at her in church...hold her hand...and recite a prayer in her favor
9. Tickle her when she is angry
10. Listen to her when she is telling you a boring story... sound interested
11. Listen to him when he is talking about technical stuff!
12. Love him harder when guys stare at you
13. Wear his T-shirts and basketball shorts around him
14. Dance slowly…in a random place...with no music... no song
15. Give her random gifts to make her smile
16. Hold his hand to help each other through life

It's the simple things that matter most!!!

Part. 5

To Every Guy…

To every guy that's said, "Sex CAN wait."
To every guy that's said, "You're beautiful."
To every guy that was never too busy to drive across town to see her...
To every guy that gives her flowers and a card when she is sick or down…
To every guy who gives her flowers just because that's how he is…
To every guy that said he would die for her…
To every guy that really would…
To every guy that did what she wanted to do...
To every guy that cried in front of her…
To every guy that she cried in front of…
To every guy that holds hands with her…
To every guy that kisses her with meaning…
To every guy that hugs her when she's sad…
To every guy that hugs her for no reason at all…
To every guy who would give his jacket up for her…
To every guy that calls to make sure she got home safe…
To every guy that would sit and wait for hours just to see her for ten minutes...
To every guy that would give his seat up...

To every guy that just wants to cuddle…
To every guy that reassured her she was beautiful no matter what…
To every guy who told his secrets to her…
To every guy that tried to show how much he cared through every word and every breath…
To every guy that thought maybe this could be the one…
To every guy that believed in her dreams…
To every guy that would have done anything so she could achieve her dreams…
To every guy that never laughed at her when she told him her dreams…
To every guy that walked her to her car and opened the door…
To every guy that gave his heart…
To every guy who prays she is happy even if he is not with her…
You are the REAL MVP!

5 Simple Steps

I was asked to write about how a man should treat a woman. First things first, BE A MAN! After saying that, men just follow these five simple steps to a relationship.

MEET

COURT

FALL IN LOVE

MARRY

STAY TOGETHER

Meet: Do you go to church? Do you go grocery shopping? A little known gem of knowledge is Barnes & Noble. Women LOVE that place!

Court: Courting means dating with the intent to marry. So, if you don't want to marry, don't go to Barnes & Noble. Go to place that have names like, "Chocolate City" or "Stilettos," or "Landing Strip".

Fall in love: After you find that special woman, loving her is next. Don't love her just a little bit. Don't love her when the ball game is off; love her always. With everything you possess. Yes, love her enough to let her play the X-Box. Now THAT is love!

Marry: Give her a real diamond ring. Give her your last name. Make sure that together you will have your own home. Marry for better or worse. Being married is a partnership.

Stay together: The hardest part of a relationship. When she gains weight from YOUR kids, stay, and love her more. When she fusses because you came in late from hanging out with your friends, don't get mad. Be happy you have someone who loves and cares about you. Remember, women are looking for the same thing men are: trust, love, financial stability, and sex are on the path to a woman's heart. Plenty of sex. Lots of sex. GOOD SEX!

With You

I want to come with you,
run away with you,
be at one with you.
To talk in the lovers language.
Talk…and never utter a word.
To look into your eyes,
to silently search your soul.
I want to come with you
in that still, small part of the night.
Can I come?

Are We Even?

If 50 plus 50 equals 100, how can U plus I equal
nothing?
When we started, we both brought 25 to the table
Because 50 was all we needed to learn.
As time went on, we increased at different speeds.
One month, I was 60 in, you were 40 in.
The next month, you were 70 and I, 30.
We finally reached the day when your 50
and my 50, shot to 100!
We took off,
our love took off.
The closer we came to tying the infinity knot.
The more the knot unraveled.
We started slipping, you down 15,
me down 35,
until the day we realized that
if we don't add our words together
to make sense,
then U, plus I, will mean zero.

That Vibe

Last night, I felt vibrations in my ear. Not the usual kind of vibes, but…different. These vibes reminded me of good times, other times, not yet times. My ear……. trembled…… last night. My ear experienced a wide variety of vibes. From one side of the scale to the next and all in between. The good sounding vibes in my ear last night…almost….made my toes curl. The vibes made me want to… gush. But I didn't, I…trickled. These vibes took me to a place I am waiting to go again, and again. These vibes gave me a moment, a stolen moment, away from the usual bland one note beat that has become every day. These vibes put color where grayness settled. If these vibes stood before me last night, I would have enveloped myself in them not wanting to come out to feel the stale, old, cold one note beat. I closed my eyes last night and let my ear guide me through the vibe. My ear danced, my ear laughed, my ear cried, at one point my ear wanted to climax from the intense vibe that was filling up every… corner…point....every 'spot' within me…….. whew… that vibe…

Tantalizing

As my hands slowly travel down the spine of your back,
I am tantalized.
As my hands caress the smooth baldness or low cut fade
of your dome, I am tantalized.
As my hands hold your hands and my eyes study the
smooth brown lines, I am tantalized.
As my hands glide across your expansive chest and palm
your breasts, I am tantalized.
As my hands find the rhythm your hips are so
wonderfully giving, I am tantalized.
As my hands trace over your chiseled countenance and
feel your smile, I am tantalized.
As my hands match the beat that your heart is giving
only to me, I am in love.

I Just Want to Take Care of You

I am up late at night completing homework
with eyes so tired.
I know you come home from work
bone weary and exhausted, real mans work.
I think about how we met.
It was so funny and trivial at best.
We sat and laughed about another female
and the way she was spewing venom, hating on males.
Your conversation was mature.
Your words were so confident.
I never thought I would have a conversation
that didn't start with "hey shawty"
and end in "ya know man."
Tonight…
you came home from work
and I looked at your face.
I told you to take a shower
while I fix your plate.
It brings me pleasure to know you are working hard for us.
It gives me pain to know how hard you work for us.
I just want to take care of you
and wrap you tight in my arms.
Every night you come home looking
like life has you drawn.
I just want to take care of you.

I want to take the burden away.
Knowing tomorrow
you will be back out there…
working… another day…

Goodness!!!

Sitting here listening to this song makes me daydream about...................... ummmmmm.................. that time. It was a Monday, a manic Monday to be exact. Work was hectic, people demanding, and time was short. I needed to take a couple of minutes and clear my mind. I closed the office door and proceeded to play one of my 'freaky' songs. You know, one of 'those' songs. The one that gets you on instant wet-wet status. Yeah, the first one was "Beautiful" by Musiq. Ohhh, that brothas voice in my ear, and those smooth vocals trickling over my already turned on body.... oohhhhh yeahhhhhh. If any man EVER got his hands on my playlist, it's on! Musiq just MAKES me feel Beautiful with this song. It takes me to a place where I can just...be. I can just be anybody, with anybody, doing anything. The place it took me to this time was a deserted beach. My fantasies are places where I want to get Freaky. Yes, capitol F Freaky! I'm sitting on the beach, enjoying the sunset, and my hat flies off my head. As I get up to run after it, I notice this man running for it also. Oh. My. Gosh! This man!! OH MY GOSH! He had to be at least 6 foot 3 inches tall. A giant compared to my 5'5" height. A short fade, well-defined muscles...made me want to lick his arm. This man was a real life vision of Mandingo. He reached

my hat before I did. So, I stopped and stood in place waiting for him to come to me. As he walked toward me, the swagger this man possessed had me instinctively clench my thighs together. The confidence he wore, whew… Jesus… Help Me! As he moved closer, I noticed the smile. His lips closed, just a smile, a sexy smile. He stands in front of me and extends my hat towards me and asks in a voice so deep I wanted to fall in and set up home, "hi, looking for this?" I wanted to say, "yes, looking for you my entire life." Then common sense prevailed, and I took my hat with a "thank you." He doesn't move. He stands there smiling, a half smile. He says, "My name is Ray, and yours?" By this time, I had completely forgotten who I was, where I was. And, AGAIN, common sense told me to say, "I'm Kim." The wind is blowing behind him and the scent of his body is making my thighs sweat.
MANNNNNNNNNNNNN!!!!!!!!!!!!!!!!! MY STUPID OFFICE PHONE RINGS!!!!!!!!! Oh well, I'll be back with another song to dream about another getaway.

Just Lay

This morning we laid and cuddled.
You, holding me, against your chest.
Amazing, how we…fit so well within each other.
I can hear your heart beating…
one…two…three…
perfectly in tune with me.
I run my fingers over your chin,
lightly, gently,
and I feel something beginning to stir.
This is not the time for that.
This is the time of stillness,
Of learning,
Of being.
This morning we laid and cuddled.

Passion

Your pleasure is my desire…
I like to watch you breathe.
It makes me more aware of the depths
of Passion I'm taking you to.
Passion.
I give you nothing to ever want for more.
The height of pleasure is Passion
which I give you completely,
never sacrificing in my quest to please you.
Passion.
From licking your naval,
your shudder makes me want to go deeper…
deeper into giving you what you want.
Passion.
What do you need?
I'm letting you feel my need.
My need to make you want me and only me.
Passion.
Your pleasure is my desire.
My desire to match your thrust one for one…
your moans one by one…
Passion.
Your cry for pleasure is my reward,
and my name on your lips is a sound so natural,
I want to hear it again.

Passion.
It's you I want to make happy…
I want you to make me happy…
Stroke me.
Feel me.
Enter me!
I don't mind if you rub a little harder…
I wish you would,
in Passion.

Especially Sexy

What makes you sexy?
Your intellect
Your mental strength
Your inner beauty
Your walk
What turns you on?
The way you dance
Your smile
The way you wear your clothes
Your sensitive eyes
Your gentle touch
The way you move through a crowd
The cut of your hair
The way you praise our Lord
The kindness in your heart
The sweetness in your kiss
The romantic in you
The precious way you see life
Your joy in giving
Your graciousness in getting
The tender way you hold me
The security I feel in your arms
The deep richness of your voice
The way you whisper my name
The well-toned muscles of your body
Just the special way you love me

I Would Love to Talk to Him

I would love to talk to him
and to hear his voice.
Is it deep?
Does it rumble?
Or is it smoothhhhhhhh?
Making me want to take a tumble…with him.
He said we can go half on a baby
and ohhhh maybe, just maybe...
Sigh…
I would love to hear his voice,
to hear how he speaks.
Is he hood?
Does he use common slang?
Or do his words flow
nicely enunciated
Proper grammar?
I really really want to hear his voice.
I wonder if the first word would make me wet?
I wonder if when can speaks
His words take me to a place...
A place of sensuality?
One day, one day,
I will hear his voice.

Sun Kissed

As I walk, looking around
the sun kissed sand, my eyes fall on him.
Tall, elegant, a beautiful poised picture
of what a Black Man should be.
I breathe in the site
because to me
he is the only living creature around.
As I walk toward the swaying swings,
my steps echoing the swinging beat of my hips,
he swings his perfectly shaped eyes toward me.
His gaze locks with mine,
our eyes intertwine,
and I impulsively want to grind.
The sun is high, and so is he.
Across the deep sandy expanse of time
he found me,
my soul mate,
the Black Man for me.

PART 2:

Black Woman

Black Woman

I am so very proud to be a Black Woman.
I am so very proud of my curves,
of the seductive slope of my breasts,
and the way I see you watching my chest
rise…and fall…
The world has tried,
tried to emulate me.
But don't they know…
original is all I can be.
Countries, generations, races
were birth from my womb,
the womb of a Black Woman!
Threats, rocks, and insults
were thrown at my skin,
the skin of a Black Woman!
And yet, and YET!
I am still here.
I am standing.
So proud, so humble,
with a spirit so free.
I am so very proud to be a Black Woman.
So very proud to be me!

CLEARING THROAT, STEPPING TO MIC

Excuse me; I have something to say!
I know I am not the cliché dime piece kinda size piece female. I know my hair is not the most luxurious 16-inch yaki flowing down my back-y. I know I cannot hold a note and my bank account is not stacked *with* notes. But let me tell you what I do know. I know I am a black woman. I am a Queen. I am a Black Queen who deserves her Black Mandingo King. I have birthed a child from between these soft thighs that give my man a rise. My heart is on display…don't abuse it because when a woman is fed up, well, you know the rest. These arms have comforted men, women, and children in the past. I have so much love to share, and so many secrets to bear. I may not be that dime piece arm candy piece, but I am a time-piece. I am the kind of woman a man marries until the end of time. I am that kind of woman who's that is in your corner when you feel alone. I am the kind of woman who will encourage her man through the down time, praying be comes back up time. I am the kind of woman that will birth your dreams as well as your children. I am a Black Queen, the forever piece.

Invisible Hurt

I'm so invisible it hurts.
I don't want to show cleavage,
I don't want to show butt cheeks,
I don't want to always talk sex,
I want to be me.
I want to be noticed for me.
For the fun loving,
non-cursing,
non-drinking,
tender soul that I am.
I feel as if I have to sell myself out to get attention.
Why?
Why should I have to go that far?
Because we, the women who still respect ourselves…
We are a dying breed.
We die daily.
We are killed by the twerking videos.
We are killed by the nude pictures.
We are killed by the foul mouth females,
who are now garnering all the attention.
We are a dying breed.
An invisible dying breed no one will notice
when we have cried the last cry and sobbed the last sob.
We are dying because we are invisible.

Who Told You!?

I can do all things!
I will do all things!

Little black girl, who told you not to?
Don't you know nations were born from the belly of a black woman?
Don't you know the struggle was made easier because of black women?

Little black girl, who told you not to speak?
Don't you know songs of uplifting and empowerment were sung by black women?
Don't you know schools and colleges were built by black women?

Little black girl, who told you that you couldn't wear that pretty dress?
Don't you know the world follows what black women choose to adorn themselves with?
Don't you know black women have achieved power from the strength of a power suit?

Little black girl, who told you not to?
You CAN DO ALL THINGS!
You WILL DO ALL THINGS!

The next time somebody tells you no, you tell them your Father in heaven told YOU,
I can do ALL things through Christ Jesus who strengthens ME!

Painting Toes

While I paint my toes, I start to reflect on life… on love… on me. What kind of me do I want to be? Have I already reached the highest pinnacle I will reach? Is there more out there for me? We all have to take time to sit and reflect, think back on things that happened in the past, making sure some of them do not get repeated.

Phone calls from friends make me smile. As I reflect back on those conversations, are they of substance, something for me to hold onto? As I reflect back on giggles shared with an invisible phone cord, will I remember why we giggled, or just the giggle?

While I sit painting my toes, my thought process speeds up to the future. I reflect back on the yet to come of my future Am I doing enough, or is there more to do? The impending events my present mind frame continuously tries to wrap around are a wrap.

I will sit here and finish my toes, thinking thoughts of thankfulness to the Most High. Thankful I am allowed to sit here and paint my toes.

Birthday Wish

Every year, my wish for my birthday is the same.
Actually, I have two wishes,
both the same.
One wish has a depth of forever,
one I whisper in everyday breath.
One I know God hears,
and every day I wake up,
He has fulfilled.
The other wish is just the same,
except the wish doesn't have a name.
I used to wish this wish for Christmas.
Then I used to wish it at the New Year
but then I realized since it will never come true,
I will use it as a birthday wish.
Birthday wishes are pure fantasy.
Birthday wishes are only for joy.
Birthday wishes are not spoken,
no words in the air
for fear they will not come true.
Now, I have reached this point in my life,
and I have wished this wish for twenty years,
I think it is safe to let this one go,
since it will never come back fulfilled.
I have always wished for a birthday date,
a man to take me out for one night.

One night just for me.
One night for me to feel spoiled,
one night for me to enjoy.
One night I can look back on,
and say thank you Jesus,
it actually came true.

PART 3:

Whimsy

OOOOO…

Oooooo, did you feel that?
I felt it as it stepped into the room.
It felt as if I became whole.
Goose bumps cascaded down my arm, my neck, my back.
It felt as if my life came into focus.
I didn't know my life had been so gray.
It felt as if the world opened up to me,
as if I had been moving in circles around myself.
It felt as if I had more strength to…be.
Ooooo, did you feel that?
It felt as if my heart skipped a beat.
It looks like LOVE has finally found me.

Dreams

I dreamed a dream of golden skies…
I dreamed a dream of open arms…
I dreamed a dream of carefree happiness…
I dreamed a dream.

I long to run and jump in the vast expanse of joyfulness.
Joyfulness that is only found beyond the rainbow.
Rainbows are near and far; I must guide my heart through the fog.
The fog of uncertainty, the fog of doubt.

I dreamed a dream of golden skies…
I dreamed a dream of open arms…
I dreamed a dream freedom…
I dreamed a dream.

I Will Never Understand....

I will never understand why we let words break
something that is supposed to be solid.
I will never understand why I have to accept all your
flaws, but am not allowed to have any of my own.
I will never understand why it was so easy to throw away.
I will never understand why my apology to you
crumbles like clay.
I will never understand why if I accept all the blame,
I'm still at fault.
I will never understand why you don't think you have
faults.
I will never understand why you think I need to grovel.
I will never understand why it was so easy for you to let
it go.
I will never understand why two people can't talk it out.
I will never understand why, if one is willing, the other
is unwilling.
I will never understand and since I don't, I will leave it
here, in these words.
Because I do understand that I am moving
on...

My Soul Cries

For the child with no mother
For the child with an abusive mother

My soul cries

For the love never found
For the love found, then lost.

My soul cries

For the family whose unity is never known
For the family whose unity, because of deceit, is gone

My soul cries

For the prayers that people are too afraid to pray
For the prayers of people led astray

My soul cries

Peaceful Calm

Whistling
Whispering
The breeze softly glides across my skin.
Softly
Gently
I feel peace slowly enter within.
Peace
Quiet
Is the air surrounding my existence.
Airy
Lightly
Is the tender breath I take in, I breathe out.
Tenderly is the life I begin…again.

Royalty

If I were a color, I would be purple.
The color of majestic royalty.
Kings and queens
from the motherland
rocked me.
Purple,
deep hued,
or light lavender.
Purple roses,
exotic,
sparse,
limited,
priceless royalty.

Brightest Unknown

We are all the same,
yet…
We are all different.
We come from worlds apart
to find we share the same spirit.
I see the blank universe before me
and I perceive a dark void left behind.
The myriad of infused colors on the horizon brighten
my corneas and open my mental capacity to take in
all that is offered to me. I look deep into the swirling
of emotions, I am allowed to envision being wrapped
around my heart and…I…won't…let…go…
When I take a chance, off balance,
my foot touches the brightest edge of the unknown.

PART 4:

Short Thoughts...

1. Age-old wisdom spawns newfound philosophy.

2. Normalcy is but a fleeting image of what reality seeks to acquire. Reality of a normal night spent with strange, unforgettable people forgotten in the morning air after a time of distant travel…

3. While the dew hangs heavy in the morning air,
   I reach over to feel a touch and remember what
   we shared.
   Last night is but a memory, a tingle in my thighs,
   dang, not again, only my finger gave me that rise!!!
   Sigh…

4. As I lay, subdued from the erotic actions of hands and bodies of the near past, I think back to what lies ahead. Will I repeat, in the future, the glorious moment we shared? Or will I let the past lie?

5. My mind wraps around rhythm and rhymes to find the time to grind out a little line. We can go high… or we can go low, low, low, low, ahhhhh, but bring it back around to the tune of taking it slow. I feel music in my bones, I feel a jones in my bones, I feel…

6. People and Questions
   I am waiting for the right question.

I am waiting for the right one to ask the right question. People and questions…

7. When you call I want my pulse to speed up! When you walk into a room, I want my breath to catch! When you say my name, I want to exhale! When you kiss me, I want to fly…

8. Songs are personal. If you have ever been allowed to see into someone's playlist, you have just been given a chance to see inside their soul and listen to their well-hidden secrets and deepest desires. Handle With Care

9. I sit back and listen,
   I sit back and groove…
   I sit back and flow with the sound of the music that is reverberating through my eardrums…
   Breathe in and breathe out, slow, don't mess up the flow.
   Bobbing heads and tapping feet, all to the rhythm of the breathing.
   I sit back and listen,
   I sit back and groove…

PART 5:

Prayers

IN THE NAME OF JESUS

In the name of Jesus, God we come before you right now, asking forgiveness for any and all sins we committed, knowing and unknowing. We ask you touch the families of terrible tragedies. Lord, please help them through their grief and please stand beside them through the recovery process. Heal the hearts of the parents who suffered loss and give them the strength to keep living and praising your Holy Name. "And we know that all things work together for good to them that love God, to them who are the called according to his purpose" (Romans 8:28). We can rest assured you are a great and just God, and ANYTHING we are given as a test is already a test overcome. You do not give us more than we can handle and we know we are worthy in your eyes to make it through. Lord, right now, please touch the hearts and minds of children who are in pain and give them peace. Erase the bad and replace it with good. Please teach the parents to guide these young souls in the way of righteousness and to follow in your footsteps. "Train up a child in the way he should go: and when he is old, he will not depart from it" (Proverbs 22:6). God, we ask this and all things in the name of your Son, Jesus Christ, Amen.

As We Hold the Hand

We hold the hand because we know we cannot stand
by ourselves without HIM.
As we move through the thin reality of life,
our lives are but a whisper in the breeze of trees.
Sometimes it takes all we can muster
to act,
to move.
We must hold on!
We cannot let go!
We have to believe that
We WILL make it up that hill,
to The One that we look towards
For help,
For wisdom,
For peace.
We hold the hand because we know we cannot stand
by ourselves…
without HIM.

Think People!

I wish more people would think on this and take heed. Some people let the outward appearance determine the soul of a person. Where some people may have extra weight on them, they may also have a light, beautiful, and worthy heart of gold. Don't let the visual physical keep you from arriving at your soulful destiny.

Men, not every woman will look like a super model. Even though the outside is appealing, remember the inside soul could be black as coal. Some women carry the extra weight not because they over eat, but because they have so much love and no one to give it to.

Women, remember, just because he doesn't have a chiseled face or twelve-pack abs, doesn't mean he is not a remarkable provider and a man of God. He doesn't need a six-figure salary to give you a good home and be a great father to your children.

Beauty is not in the face;
beauty is a light in the heart.♥

Just a Thought.......................

As single people waiting for our Boaz's and Ruth's, we need to prepare ourselves. We can't just sit here and say, "when God brings him to me" or "when God shows me her." We have to be proactive. We have to start getting ourselves together. Stop waiting on someone to come save you. Get up and get yourself together. Spiritually, financially, emotionally and physically, get ready!

1. Spiritually, by making sure you have a solid relationship with Jesus. Let God guide your steps now so when the right person comes along, you will know how to lead or follow with Godly wisdom and love.

2. Financially, by clearing up unpaid bills and your credit. No one wants a broke partner. Pay off bills or start paying on them. Get a second job if you have to. Marriage is work, so start putting in that work now.

3. Emotionally, by letting go of all the anger and bitterness from the past. Aren't you tired of being mean? Aren't you tired of crying? Then stop, and get it together. Why are you dragging past trash into a bright new future? Dump and leave it in the past.

4. Physically, by not being lazy. Walk or go to the gym. You have all these preconceived notions of who you want to marry, well, so do they. Prolong your life together by getting in shape now, so when you get married you can stay in shape together.

We can always say we are waiting, but God does not attend pity parties. He helps those who help themselves. So get up and make a move on your new relationship before it gets here. Also in the course of getting ready, you will discover how much better you feel about yourself.

Leadership Prayer

Father, we come to you today to pray for people in leadership positions. From the clergy to the White House to the schools, Lord, you are needed. We ask you to come in like a mighty rushing wind and give people back their common sense to do right. We ask you to help them to look the enemy in the eye and say no. We ask you to help them learn to call and depend on you. We ask you to guide their decision-making that affects not only them, but the many people they are responsible for. In the Holy and Wonderful name of Jesus, Amen.

About the Author

Kimberly Humphrey wrote this book as an ode to Black Men. She feels Black men are severely under-valued and unappreciated. This is her way of giving back and saying thank you.

She has one daughter and is a foster parent to three siblings. She lives in the low country of South Carolina where she founded a non-profit teen organization called Teens of Power. She was in the U.S. Navy for ten years and stationed on three different ships, the U.S.S Merrimack, U.S.S Samuel Gompers, and finally, the U.S.S Abraham Lincoln.

Kimberly received her Bachelor's in Communications from Paul Quinn College, the only HBCU in Dallas, and she received her Master's in Business Administration from the University of Phoenix. She is currently pursuing her doctorate in Management of Organizational Leadership.

www.ingramcontent.com/pod-product-compliance
Lightning Source LLC
Chambersburg PA
CBHW051848040426
42447CB00006B/753

* 9 7 8 1 9 4 4 3 1 3 0 6 7 *